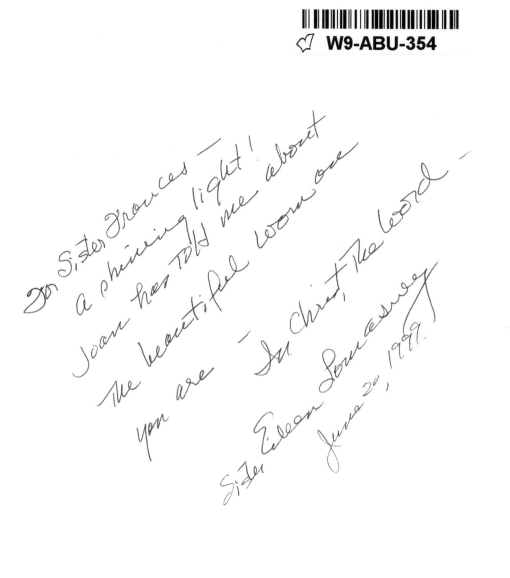

To Sister Frances —
a shining light!
Joan has told me about
the beautiful woman you
are — In Christ, The Lord —
Sister Eileen Loncassey
June 20, 1999.

Books By Eileen Lomasney

Nearing Bethlehem: A Chapbook of Christmas Poetry

For Children

My Book of The Lord's Prayer

My Book of Happiness: The Beatitudes For Children

Timmy Greenthumb

"What Do You Do With The Rest of The Day, Mary Ann?"

Two Children Who Knew Jesus

Light From Another Room

Light From Another Room

New and Selected Poems
1940 - 1994

by Eileen Lomasney

CANTICLE PRESS
LATHAM, NY
1994

Cover and art work: Marion Honors, CSJ
Design and Typesetting: Maureen Lomasney,
Tannery Creek Press, Bodega, CA 94922
Typeface: TrueType Times New Roman
Paper: Artemis Pearl Text 70 lb.
Cover stock: Tomohawk 80 lb.
Printer: Allied Reproductions, Cohoes, NY

Library of Congress Catalog Card Number: 94-94629

ISBN 0-9641725-1-8 pbk

First Edition

Grateful acknowledgement is made to the editors of the following publications
in which most of these poems first appeared: *America, Breakthrough, Delta
Epsilon Sigma Journal, The Evangelist, Inscape, Magnificat, Round Lake
Journal, Spirit: A Magazine of Poetry, The Sign, Spirited Words.*
Poems published prior to 1965 bear the name Sister Mary Ada.

I am especially grateful to Francine Dempsey, CSJ, Marion Honors, CSJ, and
my niece, Maureen Lomasney, for their personal and professional help in the
preparation of this manuscript.

Special thanks to my Religious Community, The Sisters of St. Joseph of
Carondelet, Albany Province, who made possible the publication of this
volume.

Published by Canticle Press, Latham, NY 12110-4741

We find rest in those we love,
and we provide a resting place
in ourselves for those who love us.

St. Bernard of Clairvaux

All my life I have been blessed
with the love of family and beloved
friends. This book is a Thank You
for that great gift.

E.L.

An Accidental Preface

In the beginning, there was to be no preface. The poetry, I reasoned, will stand or fall on its own – as indeed it will. But then, my niece, Maureen, who typeset the manuscript, included a letter with the galleys which changed my mind on the matter. Having lived with the poems for a while, Maureen had discerned a dimension of the collection which had eluded me. She found a story braided within the chronology of the poems, a nun's story, in this case. Not the one presented to the public in *Nunsense*, or *Sister Act*, to be sure, but rather one lived by a woman who happens to be a poet – the inside story, as it were. My Editor agreed it might be a courtesy to share the last few paragraphs of Maureen's letter with the reader at the conclusion of my introductory reflections.

Is the story necessary either for the enjoyment of, or for an evaluation of the poetry? No, it isn't. We read poetry to savour sound and sense, to enter its rhythms and cadences, to refresh the spirit, or simply for the joy of finding good words put together well. We read poetry for some of the same reasons we take up any literary genre – to discover another window on the universe, another patch of light playing in the dusty corners of the everyday, or to rediscover the adorable contours of our own lost landscapes. Sometimes we simply long to hear another human voice attempting to name the world. That is how I hope you will read these pages.

As you read, you will discover an evolution of both form and content in the poems, understandable given the time-frame covered in their writing. I tried several arrangements but in the end the chronological proved most satisfactory despite certain misgivings. My concern was this. Would the earlier poems, structured as they are in forms seldom used today, discourage the reader more comfortable with contemporary modes of writing? Modes which follow the natural rhythms and flow of human speech? The new writing brims with possibilities for me, but I make no apologies for a well-turned sonnet, a couplet or a quatrain which has been honestly honed and completed with integrity without having lost the original wonder, the "*AH!*", which surprised and set the soul ablaze in the first place.

Classical forms are an excellent foundation, indeed an education for the poet, insuring the mastery of the craft, the creation of the well-made work in the same way the principles of design serve the painter, or the rules of composition benefit the composer. The freedom to bend, break, or modify the rules is born of a good schooling in the discipline. It is important, however, that poet, painter or musician explore that freedom using it to grow, and in a very real sense, to extend Creation for all of us. Could we have come from Giotto to Van Gogh, from Mozart to Mahler, from Dante and Shakespeare to Hopkins and e.e.cummings if thousands of major and minor creators, including unheralded women, had not exercised both freedom and discipline in between? The thing is to treasure the whole of it.

Treasure the whole of it, I do, but grateful I am for even the smallest phrase which helps me to see more clearly the wonder of the world of which I am a part. No late afternoon sun in Fall or Winter has been quite the same since discovering in my girlhood Emily Dickinson's, "There's a certain Slant of light." No Spring or Summer morning more fresh than those on which I remember a line of Edith Sitwell's, "The emeralds are singing in the grasses." And all of life is sweeter because Dante emerged from that dark region through which the poet Virgil had guided him knowing he was enveloped in that great Love which "Moves the sun, and the moon, and all of the other stars." It is in that Love I read my niece's letter – and in which I write these words.

Before concluding, there are two questions I would like to anticipate. The first, why the break at 1965? The year is not purely arbitrary, but marks the time following Vatican II when we were allowed to resume our baptismal names. Poetry written between 1940-1964 was published under my religious name of Sister Mary Ada. I mention this because several poems not included here were anthologized under that name. One poem found here, *Limbo*, originally published in *America Magazine* in 1947 and anthologized several times, continues to be reprinted with its original designation. I hope this clears up the matter.

You should also know that my becoming a nun and the call to poetry were not concomitant events. The commitment to poetry came early in life on a day I remember clearly with great joy – my seventh birthday. My beloved Aunt Bert had given me two books of poetry at breakfast that morning, volumes one and two of **Poems Every Child Should Know**. Although nearly eight decades have passed since I unwrapped those treasures, I can still see the covers, their colors, the pictures, the style of lettering. I can smell the gold imprinted spines; feel the textured pages. And that was only the beginning of their magic. I took the books out to my ivy-covered corner of the wrap-around porch to read them aloud. My excitement mounted as I realized what was happening on the page as I read. Unable to contain myself, I ran into the kitchen where my Grandmother was baking, and hugging her mightily, announced, "Grandma, they sound beautiful and they make sense! I want to do that, too!" She let me point out to her the rhyming words, how they occured in just the right places for both the sense and the music to happen. Then she took a yellow pad and pencil from the kitchen cabinet saying: "Here – go try." Back on the porch I struggled until I had two "poems", and a feeling of pride and pleasure. After the birthday cake that evening, I read them to the whole family. The response, so warm and loving, set me on the way.

A few years later a beloved friend gave me a book by John Wu, titled *Beyond East and West* in which I discovered a lodestar. "Poetry," I read, "should be as simple as water in expression, and as deep as the sea in impression." I can no longer find the book, but in my mind's eye, I see those words just above center on the right-hand side of the page. They still seem an ideal worth fulfilling in a finished poem. The words of my niece which I promised at the beginning of this accidental preface brought all this, and more, to mind. It is time to share them:

Aunt Eileen,

. . . I must say that working on your book has been an absolutely wonderful, enlightening and quite emotional experience for me. It's been difficult for me to proofread because I keep getting caught up in the lyricism and beauty of the poems themselves. And I know that if I ever need to cry on cue, all I have to do is read *Limbo* — it does it every single time.

As a body of work, representative of your fascinating and deeply felt life, I feel I know you more intimately than I ever have. I also feel that your book is an *important* work for some very specific reasons, based on my own experiences as an admirer of beautifully crafted writing, as a Catholic, as a member of the same family, and as a woman.

Briefly, your experience as a nun, 'lo these many years, represents a period of history in the Church, and in the changing roles of women in society, that covers territory which no longer exists. The old black and white habits are gone; there are fewer women entering religious orders; and the reasons for entering may be quite different than they once were.

Also, not a whole lot has ever been known in the general population about the inner thoughts and feelings of women of your experience. To hear and feel the hope and love and longing in your words would be quite a revelation to many people who have a great curiosity about members of a religious order who took vows as you did at such a young age.

People will read your collected works and see you mature as a writer and woman of great faith and humanity. They will also see that joy, exultation and the freedom to trust in God, based on the strength of your personal experience, is linked to the vows you took – even before you could fully know their impact.

This kind of freedom of spirit, or *joie d'esprit*, within carefully drawn lifestyle boundaries, will be a welcome revelation to many people who may feel constricted in their own lives. It may provide encouragement to those who may have felt that vows could only inhibit thought rather than act as an empowering environment in which the spirit is truly liberated to love God, Nature and all of humanity.

I would love to see **Light From Another Room** enjoy the kind of appreciative audience it (and you) richly deserves. If I can do anything to encourage that process, please let me know. In the meantime, thank you for giving me this opportunity to spend such a wonderful time in the intimate quarters of your heart.

Much love, and always,
Maureen

Do you wonder why I wanted to share this with you?

E.L.
Windy Hill
Ballston Lake, New York
Feast of the Holy Angels,
September 29, 1994

Contents

1965-1994

1940-1965

Just to be is a blessing.
Just to live is holy.

Rabbi Abraham Heschel

The Child Who Brought Me
One Small Rose

I taught him how to write his name,
Some nursery rhymes, a children's game.

And when he brought me one small rose
He brought more heaven than he knows.

For woven with the rose's scent
His wordless love was eloquent.

And he, contented with my smile,
Had skipped away. But for awhile

I could not stir, nor could I say
How love possessed me all that day.

1940

1

Wedding Night: Mary and Joseph

Snow white blossoms at her heart
And stars about her hair.
(Joseph cannot find the words
To put into his prayer).

All her raiment too, is white
And white her little hands.
(Joseph cannot think beyond
the heaven where she stands).

Now she takes his candlestick
And puts it on the sill.
(Like his love it circles her,
All radiant and still).

Joseph vows to keep for love,
(Love has a magic art),
Shining stars about her hair —
White blossoms at her heart.

1941

Against Despair

You are a Treasure, Lord, beyond all price.
I needs must tell you as the pledge I lay
Against that bitter and regretful day
When I might well deny You more than thrice.

And lest I be as so much sifted wheat,
Oh, pray no grain by any wind shall blow
Beyond the magnet of your eyes, or go
Outside the reach of pinioned hands and feet.

Or should I sell you, and the price be set
At thirty silver pieces, more or less,
Oh, let me not forget in my distress
The heart I bartered will receive me yet.

1942

The Fifth Station: Simon of Cyrene Helps Jesus To Carry His Cross

I, Simon, man of the world
have chosen the better part:
better his cross on my back
than his eyes on my heart.

1943

Explaining Purgatory

Leaf by wary leaf will Spring unfold
The beauty that is gathered to her heart.
Drop by dewy drop the liquid gold
Of sun is laid on petals blown apart.

Day on constant day the lovelight grows
Until a lamp is ready for the night.
Word by singing word will joy disclose
The hidden secret well-springs of delight.

So by ways as merciful as these,
Because the heart may break of ecstasy,
Flame on cleansing flame the faint soul frees
To God's embrace and Love's eternity.

1946

Meditation on a Painting
**(*Virgin of the Rose-Bower* by
Stephen Lochner 1400?-1451)**

You are the Butterfly:
She is the Rose —
Petals uplifted
For your repose.

You are the Nightingale:
She is the Nest —
Nurturing Mother,
Home where you rest.

You are the Grain of Wheat:
She is the Field —
Snowily beautiful,
Bearing full Yield.

You are the Word of God:
She is God's Song.
May poor poets sing you
As time is long.

1946

Limbo

The ancient greyness shifted
Suddenly and thinned
Like mist upon the moors
Before a wind.
An old, old prophet lifted
A shining face and said:
"He will be coming soon.
The Son of God is dead;
He died this afternoon."

A murmurous excitement stirred
All souls.
They wondered if they dreamed —
Save one old man who seemed
Not even to have heard.

And Moses standing,
Hushed them all to ask
If any had a welcome song prepared.
If not, would David take the task?
And, if they cared,
Could not the three young children sing
The Benedicite, the canticle of praise
They made when God kept them from perishing
In the fiery blaze?

A breath of spring surprised them,
Stilling Moses' words.
No one could speak, remembering
The first fresh flowers,
The little singing birds.

Still others thought of fields new ploughed,
Or apple trees,
All blossom boughed.
Or some, the way a dried bed fills
With water
laughing down green hills.
The fisherfolk dreamed of the foam
On bright blue seas.
The one old man who had not stirred
Remembered home.

And there He was,
Splendid as the morning sun, and fair
As only God is fair.
And they, confused with joy,
Knelt to adore —
Seeing that He wore
Five crimson stars
He never had before.

No canticle at all was sung.
None toned a psalm, or raised
A greeting song.
A silent man alone
Of all that throng
Found tongue —
Not any other.

Close to His heart,
When the embrace was done,
Old Joseph said,
"How is your Mother,
How is your Mother, Son?"

1947

God Was So Merry

God was so merry on the morning
He planned to make the swallows and the larks,
The bob-o-links, the orioles, the sparrows,
And all the rest that fill His leafy parks.

He was so happy fashioning the feathers,
The tiny heart, the wing-span and the throat,
The brain, the bright enchanting movements,
Each separate song and every perfect note.

He dreamed with joy of days a boy would listen
To hear a robin christen morning's air
And stop to thank his Father with a whistle —
That morning and the robin found him there.

1948

The Well of Beauty

A canticle of color,
A symphony of sound,
Asks the eager-hearted
"Where is beauty found?"

The liturgy of seasons,
The rhythm of the skies
Reads like Wisdom's Primer
Furnishing replies.

Music brings us answers,
So do trees and stones.
Beauty fills the universe
As marrow fills our bones.

Beauty will attend us
At birth, through life and death
If we can hear the singing
Woven with our breath.

All syllabled creation
Spelleth last and first:
"The Word is beauty's well-spring.
O come, all you who thirst."

1948

There is a Hearth at the End of the World

There is a hearth where great good hearts
Make merry all together,
And never mind a ticking clock,
Or ever mind the weather.

Where every guest that happens in
Is sister, friend, or brother.
All bring stories, or a song
To sing with one another.

Our Father keeps the fire bright:
It glows on shining faces.
Our Mother hustles in and out
Forever saving places.

From North and South, from East and West,
All roads that come are narrow —
But Father has such anxious eyes
He numbers every sparrow.

He watches all the livelong night:
She prays against the weather.
They will not rest till all good hearts
Are safely home together.

1949

Bedtime Story for Christmas Eve

Once upon a time,
(I've heard)
God whispered to a little girl
His only Word —
The same One that He said
In the beginning,
Before there was a world at all,
Or beast or bird,
Or any sinning.
And all because
Before time was
He said,
"My Word is beautiful;
My Word is true.
I'll make someone
To tell Him to."
(And that's the reason
He made you!)

No chime
Nor bell
Announced the time,
But Gabriel
came down
Into the town
of Nazareth
to ask this child
If she would hear
This Word,

Ineffably dear,
That we might share
God's happiness.
And she said, "Yes."

And no one knew in Nazareth
That He came down
Like rain that falls
On snowy fleece
And hushed Himself
Beneath her breath
And wrapped Him
In her body's peace.
Oh, He was not afraid at all
To trust Himself to limbs
Or hair,
Or nose, or ears,
Or mouth, or eyes
He didn't need in Paradise.
Though they were darling, sure,
And fair,
And purer far
Than any other's
But like His Mother's.

And now the Word is ours alone.
In human flesh and blood and bone
We've cradled Him.
Nor Cherubim,
Nor Seraphim
Shall ever know
As we know Him.

While here for each of us to keep
Is God's own loving,
And His deep
Wide mercy, like a sea.
His wisdom and His purity,
His justice, shining like a star,
And all things beautiful that are
Or that will ever be,
Because He said,
"Who seeth Me,
Seeth My Father, too."
And it is true!

1950

The Juliet Theme in Tchaikovsky's Overture

Almost lullaby it is:
the first May violets,
the velvet wings
of nightingales —
or, ". . . is it the lark,
is it the lark that sings?"
sweet in the violins,
soft in the cello's strings?

>   hearing her heart cry low, cry low,
>   the violins know where to go —
>   rocking, rocking
>   to-and-fro
>   from childhood into womanhood.
>   Not too quickly,
>   not too slow . . .
>   the violas have understood
>   how innocence and passion could
>   be counterpoint in her —
>   (they were.)

Rock, oh rock her heart to sleep . . .

>   The cymballed swords,
>   like crashing hate,
>   will come too soon,
>   and peace too late
>   to teach her wisdom,
>   (how to lose the life we keep).

Rock, oh rock her heart to sleep . . .

The heartbreak is
this heavenly reach
of human longing
lacking speech:
of human longing
caged like birds —
though flutes are searching
for the words.

Rock, oh rock her heart to sleep.

Sing sweetly, sweetly violins.
Sing lullaby against the dark
that knows no nightingale
or lark.
Only the tolling of a bell
for Juliet. Sleep well,
dear child, sleep well . . .
But her brave soul is up and gone
To find him
in a fairer dawn.

Oh, music that has reconciled
the loving woman and the child.

1952

When David, The Psalmist, Sings

He has framed a new music on my lips, a song of
praise to our God. To fill all that stand by with
reverence. **(Psalm XXXIX:4)**

When David sings new music made of praise
And passion perfected, to God, his Song,
(His heart, a contrite child within him, strong
With noble purpose, tutored in God's ways),
His voice is lifted from a blaze
Of human love kindled by listening long
Where Wisdom whispers, "Fill the hungry throng."
So he will sing God's mercy all his days.

So he will sing, while choir on chanting choir
Still echo words of David. Each singer brings
A new voice, movement even — fingertips,
Eyes, ears, heart and mind — all singing with desire
And yearning to praise God. When David sings,
" — be witness, Lord, I do not seal my lips!"

1953

After Night Rain

The sweet air:
the freshened trees . . .
my morning heart
is on its knees.

1954

Long After Auschwitz

Ten years ago, at least.
I saw a picture in the *New York Times*
of one small dark-eyed child of five or six
with hands upraised before a bayonet
as if his head were hoary with a hundred crimes.

Old men were in the picture, too:
old men in rags which
might have fit them once
before they were all starved to skeletons.

I can't forget those old men, nor
their look of helpless grieving —
as if they'd seen
the ultimate misery — and yes,
beyond believing,
the last aloneness of the living dead
who have no memory of hope
and are too numbed to dread.

I can't forget those old men
but they are not the ones I dream of:
they do not wake me weeping
in the night.

It is the child that wakes me
all these years:
the child I bruise my hands for
on the barbed wire fence

and pound my all-too-helpless fists
against the hulking guard —
wrestling him in nightmares
for his bayonet.

I've tried and tried to reach the little boy —
to gather him,
just as his mother would,
and kiss the terror
from his great dark eyes:
to fold him soft,
and sing him lullabies:
    "Raisins and Almonds", or,
    "Shake the little dreamland tree,
    and down come pretty dreams for thee . . ."

I'd smooth his beautiful hair
and tell him not to be afraid:
that he can play tomorrow
in the sand
or paint a picture, if he likes,
bright with skyhigh rainbows — red
and green,
blue and yellow-gold
splashed all over
a whole wide
rainbow world.

1955

Finding a Dead Swallow

It must have been its maiden flight —
so small, so tiny were its bones:
its feathers little more than down.
I found it on a heap of stones.

How brave had been the little heart!
The wings still wide, still poised. The beak
wide open, too. Its wounded head
bent back. I touched it to my cheek.

Not that any life was there
my touch could heal, or mend, or save —
No tears to shed for one thus dead:
I laid him in a shallow grave.

So brief a life: so small a song.
He tried to fly as all birds do.
No tears — but oh, I cannot name
the strange, small loneliness I knew.

1956

21

An Autumn Walk

Oh, Love, look through my eyes with me.
Oh, Love, look through my heart.
This beauty, if I look alone,
Will break my bonds apart.

The hills are Persian carpeted,
The west is flaming gold,
And one more branch of crimson leaves
My heart could never hold.

The children came and took my hand.
We scuffed a golden track —
(Oh, Word of God, be child for me
Against my turning back.)

The children tumbled in the leaves
And laughing, ran away . . .
Some of my heart went home with them
Into the dying day.

The quiet comes: the blue smoke curls
From hearths where windows shine —
(Oh, Love, be strong as death in me
Or I could wish one mine.)

Oh, Love, look through my eyes with me
Or turn my heart to stone . . .
I cannot love your lovely world
And love it all alone!

1959

Sitting Next to a Child at a Concert

The programme read, you settled in your chair.
We talked a bit until the instruments
Set up a moment's clamor, then were tense.
The maestro motioned and we went from there
Into a world of wonder, as if tossed
By golden waves upon a golden shore.
And though I'd come unto this place before
I had not known how many dreams I'd lost.

I had not known, but when I looked at you
Your eyes were closed. I could not say a word
Of what I'd found, although I knew you heard
The counterpoint that dreams make: yours were new.
Contentedly I hugged the old ones — calms
Of loving round me, hearing you hum Brahms.

1961

On the Feast of St. Clare

This is a golden day,
My lady Clare,
Shining with clean, clear light
Like your golden hair.

The blue sky sings,
The white clouds smile,
And the green-gold grass,
For a little while,
Wears dew in rainbows
Under the trees
That sift the sunlight
Into these
Small pools of gold
That no man's purse
Can buy or hold.

And no man's purse
Can give delight
Like God's most beautiful
Gift of light:
Light of Wisdom:
Light of Day:
Light of stars
On Christmas hay.

And the light that shines
On your young face
Lifted in joy
And glad with grace
As Francis clips
Your golden hair
And you are God's —
Forever,
Clare!

1958

Reading a Fairy Tale to a Little Girl

The book brimmed bright with fairy tales,
Like wonder brimming in her look.
My heart in quiet looked at her,
Although I read the picture book.

"Poor Beast, poor Beast! He's really kind . . .
Not ugly in his heart . . ." she said.
    (Oh, Beauty, Beauty, Beauty's child,
    who speak so truly in her stead,

    once on a time, someone I loved
    told me that fairy tales were true;
    "They'll make you wise . . ," he said. I know
    his wisdom when I look at you!).

"I hope it comes out right for him . . .
Will Beauty understand?"
"She does," I said, "and she is good —
You needn't worry." But my hand

Turned all the pages slowly now
(I saw her joy, her silken hair),
Knowing beyond the story's end
I would not have her with me there.

1962

The Crow I Heard This Morning

The crow I heard this morning
Said I was alive.
He did not know he said it.
He did not contrive
This raucous way of rousing
My senses, nor derive

His pleasure thus. But hearing
His caw within my bones
Wakened me to glory
Only morning owns.
That sound was in my memory
Sharp as little stones.

And he unearthed bright mornings
From a golden land
Where, like a thing enchanted,
The child I was would stand
Waist-high in tall grasses
Holding summer's hand!

1963

1965-1994

There is some secret stirring in the world,
A thought that seeks impatiently its word.

Thomas Lovell Beddoes

Watching a Jet at Sunset

Coming from school
    and taking care
to let my heart
    look everywhere
I saw a jet
    skim
        quiet
            air.

The sky was blue
    and clean of clouds
while silence wrapped
    in light-gold shrouds
the wide world and
    the wider
        sky
except for one
    half-uttered
        cry
of wonder
    frought with loving
        awe
before the glory
    that I saw.

The jet curved up
    and caught
        the light
of rosegold fire —
    ALIVE
        and bright

as if it were
        a homing dove
its breast aflame
        with yearning
                love.

It soared away
        in soundless
                air . . .
Perfection
        left me lonely
                there.

1966

Having a Pillow is Not All

Having a pillow is not all:
having a bed . . .
Bitter they both may be
as tears, or bread.

And who has wine to pour,
or loaf to break,
goes hungry in the banquet hall
if none will take.

But who with love may give
what love will share —
content shall rest
both heart and head . . .
and anywhere!

1966

By the Gates of Paradise

When I was young I couldn't believe
The awful thing that happened to Eve.

"How could a woman," I used to say,
Gamble her heaven and earth away

For a bit of fruit of doubtful taste
And a glorious garden gone to waste?"

Time, the tutor, goes by, alas . . .
And Eve looks out of *my* looking-glass!

1970

In October

When green-boughed firs and golden maples lift
Their arms in light above the sumac's flame,
And that clear blue October owns for skies
Covers the world like love, I call your name.

I call down corridors of leaves: up hills —
Blue hills you loved, across the silver lakes
That mirror heaven's glory with their own.
I only hear the echo silence wakes.

But when the dusk and violet shadows fall,
Luminous peace sings in the hallowed air.
Nearer my heart than hands, or eyes, or voice —
It is your soul singing beside me there!

1971

Swimming At Dusk in the Sacandaga

The family have gone in —
it's suppertime
and all the world is heather-
blue with stillness:
only the water lapping stones
on shore, the liquid sounds
of water slapping little boats
tethered to the pilings
for the night.
Only that small
and, oh, most musical
trickling
of the water
when I turn
or lift my arm
to cut my passage
with a backward stroke.

ALL,
all is clean —
and kind:
the sky,
the far blue Adirondack
hills
that bless my eyes,

and I —
I, too, am clean,
am kind,
and full of certain music,
certain praise
for such a world,
for this good element
I move in with such ease —
as though my limbs
have been anointed
with sure grace
to be most beautiful
and fine.

How like God's love
the water is!

1972

A Prisoner of Sparrows

The feeder is frozen over
from the storm last night
so here I sit — a prisoner
of sparrows come for crumbs
I've scattered on the sill.
For when I raise my cup, or even
move my finger half an inch,
they're off . . .
I've lost them to the sky.
They'll never finish breakfast
this way — nor will I!

1974

Chrysalis

The next time Doubt,
like death,
sews up my Spirit
in a shroud
of dark
unknowing,
leave me,
Lord of my life,
memory of this new
and yellow
butterfly
filling its wings
with air
in this good world
of April
in the morning.

1975

Children in the Snow are Dancing

Three children in the snow
are dancing
while flakes fall,
and falling, swirl
soundless
in a soundless world.
Joyously the children whirl
round and down
and up — and then
flurry out
and back
again:
tumble down in pure delight
of seeing fairy flakes alight
on mittens
and on snowsuit sleeves.
Even the youngest one perceives
the flakes as wonderful.
The others look and marvel, too.
"Can things like this be really true?"
their wonder asks.

From here behind the window glass
My heart cries out: "They are – they are
as true as any bird, or star . . .
But they are lost
in stars and flowers
made of frost.

I'll not intrude one window tap
to break the spell
their wonder weaves
as they peruse a fragile map
of fairyland
held in the cupping
of a hand.

A minute passes —
a sudden gust, and then
they've taken up the dance
again!

1976

Shall I See You Again?

Shall I see you again?
Will it be as it once was?
Will the long darkness lift
In the light of your eyes?

Will your smallest of gestures
Dismiss the last shadows —
Revealing a world
Too fair to surmise?

Will you stand even taller
Than once in my girlhood
When heroes wore haloes
Without pride, without shame?

Will I hear, as I once heard,
Your voice through the tumult
Though you call softly —
And only my name?

Long since, I've forgiven
Your dying at all
(Without a goodbye
Or a word of amends).

And I've walked in the world
With purpose and ease.
I have joyed in my work:
I have treasured my friends.

But let the white snow fall
On a world hushed, as now —
Or a passage of music
Surprise me . . . ah, then

(Though time should have dried them),
Unbidden tears fall . . .
Will it be as it once was?
Will I see you again?

1976

I Never Wondered Why My Mother Sang

I never wondered why my Mother sang
When I was small — it was so usual:
Like waking to the light, or to the warm
(And oh, most wonderful), smell of bread on
Mornings when she baked. Her singing seemed
To go with baking, and with scrubbing floors,
Or hanging out the clothes on sunny days.
I never wondered, but I marvel now.

I marvel at the courage of her song —
For years were lean: the living hard to earn
Between the wars. My Father worked two jobs
To feed us then (and keep the boys in shoes!) . . .
Maybe she sang for this: that he was strong
And good, and that he loved us all that much —
Or, that he kissed her sometimes when she sang.
I never wondered . . . but I know, I know!

1977

Notes for an Exhibit of Apple Seeds
(Museum of Natural History, A.D. 3899)

An ancient legend tells us of these seeds
that there are others, wind-tucked long ago
in crevices along the northern hills
which still may germinate, should sunlight probe
the smog again some future time in Spring.

The legend may be true. Some hope it is.
Still others go so far in prophecy
They say we will see trees with blossoms —
even fruit.
Vain hope? Or dreams derived from poetry
once bound in books? Such lines, perhaps, as those
describing how the poet walked at Eastertide
through woods — imagining the blossomed boughs
as hung with snow.

1978

Christmas Eve, 1978

The carillons are calling from the spires:
The carolers are coming through the snow.
And all the stars — the very stars are singing
The song an angel taught them long ago.

We know that music, too: we know its meaning:
Its tidings of great joy: the breach it mends
Between ourselves and heaven . . . Glory
In the highest, and peace to all God's friends.

    — but Father, oh, Our Father hear us!
    the song dies in our throats
    or falters
    on a note
    of grave uncertainty.
    We're out of tune for carols —
    running out of rhyme
    with what the stars are singing:
    with what the bells are ringing.
    We cannot sing in time
    when headlines shout

        of war
        of death by fiat
        and by crime — in-
        cluding hunger . . .
        hear the children cry
        out from a thousand places.

Teach us to feed them, Father,
to kiss their tear-stained faces
before we finger blame
(wrongly or rightly),
or let ourselves off lightly.
Forgive us, Father, for ourselves
and for our world —
in Jesus' name!

"Why do you think My Child, My Son,
came ever so weak and small?
why did His mother bear Him
there in the cattle stall?"
"Why did He flee to Egypt?
why was Joseph there —
if not to do whatever he could
and guard with a father's care?"

"The questions are hard and endless
(freedoms bring wounds that smart),
but the lion shall lie with the lamb someday . . .
and the answers are in your heart!"

The carillons are calling from the spires:
the carolers are coming through the snow.
Lift up your hearts and sing . . .(the stars are singing) —
OUR GOD IS WITH US — and His Love we know!

1978

45

The Women and The Stone

We were worried about the stone
from the beginning.
We saw how Joseph,
Nicodemus,
and the others
strained
every muscle
setting it in place —
how flushed they were of face.
That final thud
had echoed in our bones.

We women know of stones:
the stone in the heart,
in the breast,
in the brain:
the stone in the throat,
in the arms and the womb.
All of these stones
are the stone of His tomb —
as the weight of all sorrow,
all pain
and all loss
is the weight of His body
hung
on the cross.

Oh, who'll come to move it,
to lift it,
to take it away
so we may go in
to see Him
again!

The morning stars were shining
when we left our lodgings
and hurried through the darkness
in the streets —
uneasy, lest we wake unfriendly sleepers.
Suppose they open shutters,
shout —
    "What are those women doing at this hour?"
suspect our destination,
send word up to the priests
that we were out
to steal the body of the Lord away?
We'd pounded spices in the mortars
half the night
so we might reach the tomb
by break of day . . .
so, miserable and frightened,
we kept on.
We would not, could not, stay away,
or hide — as some thought wise.
Safely,
we reached the Eastern Gate
just as the light,
(still soft and gray),
touched Golgotha
and seemed to smooth,
like love,
the scars
away.
We paused as in a dream we'd waken from
to find it all untrue.

But we had work to do.

Off to the West
the morning stars were dying.
Birds sang: trees
were radiant with rose-gold
tongues of light.
Then
on the garden path a moan
escaped us —
what about the stone?
"Who'll roll away the stone for us?" we cried.
To come so far,
And then to be denied?

We did not comprehend at first
the great stone set aside,
the grave cloths folded neatly
and left inside.
Here was a mystery —
and we were full of questions,
full of dread.
"Seek Him among the living,"
said the angel,
"not the dead!"

You know the story's ending
written down by friends
(Matthew and Mark, Luke,
the beloved John . . .)
the wonder never ends:
the mystery goes on . . .

the garden of this world transfigured,
nor life, nor death the same —
as when He spoke to Mary . . .
and called her by her name!

1980

48

They Took Down Our Hill
This Morning

Where will the birds go now? What will they do?
Eggs, still in the nests: nests still in the trees,
And the trees snapped off in a swath like these —
The squirrel's house down, and the owl's house, too!

The chipmunk had hidden her young so well . . .
So had the rabbit — her burrow is near
And her litter has dropped this time of the year.
Was she feeding her young when the great oak fell?

Dawn was as soft as a small child's kiss:
The first robin sang while the sky was still gray —
Then rose-gold, honey-gold light of the day
Washed over the world as in Genesis.

But men were here early with yellow machines:
Chain saws, and back-hoes, and earth-moving gear
To take down our hill in the Spring of the year.
Wounds in the earth are not all that it means

For the newly alive, the smallest of all
The young in the holes, or nests in the trees.
Couldn't we spare one summer for these?
Couldn't death wait . . . at least until Fall?

1980

How Magical It Was

How magical it was to lie
beneath those fresh-and-forest-
fragrant branches of that tree
on hushed and sleepy Christmas afternoons.
We'd brought it from the woods
just yesterday, and here it was
transformed by miracles of love
(imagine!), even as we slept,
with rainbows shimmering on balls and bells
and flowers made of light.
I thought my heart would break of beauty —
or delight.
Oh, I could see clear back to Bethlehem,
and yes, foreword to heaven
from beneath that tree.

As shadows fell I'd put each perfect toy
back in its proper place —
just as I'd seen it from the darkened hall
when I could scarcely breathe for wonder:
could not speak for awe . . .
seeing the whole before particulars.

There was the Manger in its special space,
the animals, the star,
the Holy-happy-birthday child asleep
in golden light and on the golden straw.
And very near, the bye-low-baby doll
in softest pink and white.

And games, of course, and books . . .
my Saint was bountiful with books.
They were enchanted and would come alive
even as I read them (or were read to
if the words were hard).
And once there was a sleigh: and once . . .
a unicorn.
And always in the stocking,
down in the very toe
beneath an orange and some nuts,
three shiny pennies for my very own!

Whoever weaves this magic for a child
most surely knows what love is: love
is saving-up, is sacrifice, is playful
and inventive: prone
to giving with largesse: holds back
no energy, but gives the heart's caress
with everything it proffers: minds no expense
of time, or trouble: squanders joy:
cares mightily that pennies
(three and shiny), be
where they'll be looked for every year —
that was a ritual with me.

I've loved a thousand children;
tried to teach them whose
great love all truly-love is part of:
whose is the heart of
all of the magic found beneath love's tree.
And yet, I have no child
to pour this love and magic out on
as it was poured on me.
I've minded sometimes:
sometimes heard my heart say
all is well, and as it should be.

Then kindly comfort comes
to touch the harp my faith keeps ready
for a song.
I send its music happily along
into the Noosphere to save it for some child
somewhere, who wonders about stars,
and likes to trace the crystal patterns
etched in frost,
or simply watches snowflakes falling
in the winter dusk.

No love is lost:
No love is ever lost.
I leave some for that child,
that little child alone —
and some for you
who read it in my poem.

1981

Christmas in a Troubled Time

Shall we argue of translations —
"Peace on earth, to men of good will,"
of "Peace, good will toward men"?
Whatever the words
could Your angels
sing them over, and over,
and over again?

Should we puzzle about times?
Was this the actual day?
And when
did the Wise Men get there?
Was it snowing
in Bethlehem?

And all of the pretty legends —
what of them?
Should they trouble us, too?
Even our fairy tales are true
beyond whatever the words declare.

Should we despair
because of larger questions
haunting us from headlines
and the news?
Take any one you choose:
"No room" for refugees (like You)!
No food for half of all our children:
No peace when nations arm for war . . .

What was Your coming for?
To die? Not just to die.
"I AM THE WAY," You said.
You walked our roads,
You broke our common bread,
worked with Your hands.
You wept —
(A friend's death made you weep):
You needed sleep.

You blessed our children,
healed our sick, and kept
a time for prayer —
would even make
a time for weddings.
You told those fishermen
who'd toiled all night, to toss
their nets in on the right
for quite a catch —
to make up for their loss.
Last of all, You'd take
care of Your Mother's future
from the cross.

This is the Way You marked.

And so we turn
to Your beginning in our world;
come to Your manger bed to learn
to reach our hands
out to our neighbor's hands:
to break our bread and pass it
in Your name:
to gather up our children,
warm and very dear,
and sing them lullabies
just as Your Mother sang —
that love may pass
from heart to human heart . . .
to chase away the dark —
and let Your star shine clear!

1981

Pinwheels
(Remembering Aunt Bert)

First, you take a paper square:
Cut it so — from here to there:

Take each corner: fold it in:
Fasten firmly with a pin:

Push the pin into the stick —
And there's your pinwheel! Hurry quick!

Catch the breeze:
Run down the block —

I'll be waiting by the rock . . .

> I'll be waiting,
> little girl,
> while you give
> your wheel
> a whirl.
> I'll be watching
> as you run,
> joyful,
> in the morning
> sun . . .
> seeing how
> your golden
> hair
> bounces
> in the April
> air:

how your legs
weave in and
out.

Halfway down
I'll hear you
shout —
and when you turn
your head
to see
if I'm still
here,
Oh, I will
be . . .

but I will be
remember-
ing
another child,
another
Spring,
and One
who taught me,
for love's sake,
the very things
I help you
make.

Someday you'll learn from history books:
You'll read the *New York Times*.
Perhaps you'll learn the discipline
That comes from making rhymes
To house your thoughts as musically
As Sunday morning chimes.

I hope you learn Theology:
I hope you learn to dance:
I hope you learn geography
In Italy and France.

Study Greek, and Latin, too:
Astronomy, and art . . .
Pursue pure science if you will —
But don't neglect the heart!

      Oh,
      don't forget
      when you have grown
      to pass along
      the things
      you've known
      to someone small
      and dear
      like you —
      to whom
      the whole wide world
      is new:
      how to make
      a pinwheel,
      a paper doll,
      a kite —
      (and fly it, too,
      my darling),

for this is how
delight
is saved
among the sorrows
through years
of come
and
gone,
and how
we nurture
wonder
to feed
the future
on.

◆　◆　◆　◆

Back already? Was it fun?
Yes, I know how fast you run:

Yes, I saw your pinwheel twirl
Like butterflies . . . a pretty swirl

Of yellow ones, my darling dear . . .
Or so it seemed to me from here.

1982

Between the Road and the Ditch

Clouds of blue flowers,
chicory, Queen Anne's lace:
blessing my eyes in traffic
with pure and amazing grace!

1983

The Gift Was So Immaculate
(Golden Jubilee 1937-1987)

The gift was so immaculate, so clean
and freshened at the source: was given
with such trust, and (as we know now),
with largesse — the Giver being bountiful
beyond our finite ways of measuring such things.
The gift was Time.
How could we know how much of it was ours?
How do we know how much of it we've left?
From past experience we know it will have wings —
but nothing more except that it is all surprise
and, in a way,
a most divinely merciful and tender teasing.
Life holds her counsel on the subject: will not say
if what is yet to come
be difficult or pleasing
either to our aging bodies or our ageless minds.
We only know it comes inexorably on
in seconds, minutes, hours turning swiftly to the hum
of days
we will accept, embrace, and ultimately fill
with love — (oh, please, with love),
and certainly with praise.
Filled, too, with tested faith, and hope — that precious
hope who really sleeps quite well (to paraphrase
Peguy), and rises every morning
like a little girl and says her prayers
with a new look shining in her eyes.
Yes, it is all surprise.

But there is precedent for pausing to remember:
to celebrate a time like this. There in Leviticus
God said: "The year of Jubilee is sacred —
and freedom is its work . . ."
Let us remember then.

Remember, yes, how very young we were:
how little of our lives we'd used in living
before that blue September day
we rang the bell and waited, asking to come in:
to give our lives back to the Giver. How in a sudden
quirk, or twist, in our whole mode of being
we found ourselves immersed in rules
we hardly dreamed existed. St. Joseph's Day in March . . .
Spring in the air, but fresh snow on the ground:
they cut our hair,
swathed us in serge and linen
stiffened with penitential starch —
or so it seemed. But how the chapel shone!
How marvelous the music was: the mighty organ
rolling in echoes from the vaulted ceiling
while bells behaved like children
tumbling out of school — the greater and the lesser
pealing with abandon. And then the pure, exquisite
voices of our sisters rinsing the incensed air
with canticles of joy. Magnificat!
It seemed like heaven there.
And yet . . . did not our heads feel numb?
Did not our shoulders ache?
Our mothers, surely, even our fathers wept.
These from a thousand memories we could have waked:
a thousand memories we might have kept.

The rest will keep —
tied in the bundles of our pilgrim years.
Today we hoist them, hug them, smooth them, bring them up
and lay them on the altar with the bread and cup:
work of our hands, the prayers our hearts have prayed:
times of our gladness: the times we were afraid:
the soul's dark night: the cloud of our unknowing:
joy in our friendships: and the pain —
the human pain, of growing
into wholeness . . .

But this is not the end, my sisters. The sweet earth
turns: her creatures sing as in that bright
beginning
when Wisdom played before Him every morning
(as she tells in Proverbs), with delight.
She was enchanted with the world, with life itself:
her spool of days
unwinding even as ours do. Take heart:
the gift is given still —
still comes immaculate and clean: still freshened
at the source so we might fill
it daily up with love — (oh, please, with love),
and certainly . . . with praise!

1987

After the Funeral

How easily we talked —
telling in turn our stories
from the cairn of years.
And how we laughed
remembering the tricks
he'd played on Mom, his smelly pipe,
his Mr. Fix-it jobs that went awry.

Like yesterday my wounded feelings welled
as freshly as the day'd I'd bet him
five whole cents, a solid nickel, on the Yanks
to win the Series. They had lost:
my first encounter with the cost
of betting, and it hurt.
He put his hand out for the coin —
his *own* child's coin! How *could* he?
But he did. "It means your word,"
he said. "You cannot take your word back
once it's pledged." His voice was kind,
but there it was: the nickel handed over
with regret.

Supper over, and the dishes done,
he called me to his chair:
"Here's a quarter, Honey. Shall we
go down for cones?" A quarter? Five
whole times my nickel! A hundred
times my loss! No reference, though.
He simply took my hand
and we walked down the block.

The lump still comes
through half a century
of layered life
learning his fatherhood.

Well, it went on like that for hours.
We ate and drank, warming the kitchen
and each other with his love. No one
shed a tear. We saved those
for the pillow later. My own eyes
hot and sore, the salt tears flow.
Oh, Daddy hold me. Teach me again,
and tell me,
because I need to know:
how do we learn, my Father,
to let a Father go?

1987

Here is a Mystery of Peace

Here is a mystery of peace:
I am in my house and loving it —
walls, windows, floor and furniture,
green plants growing in the light that blesses
everything it touches: books and baskets of bright
yarn, paintings, and simple stones gathered on
my walks. And where the shadows fall is beautiful.

The dappled shadows dance as branches lift and fall
beyond the window where a maple flames, a pine
dips needles in green-gold. It is October.
I have been working with my hands, am tired now
and am content to look, to savor silence,
savor peace, and wonder how peace comes.

I only know that something wonderful is here:
not beauty only, nor only silence — Mozart,
Mahler are at home here. Is peace content
of mind or heart? This pleasant room? The dying
year? The light? Or is it a sacrament whose elements
I see and touch and never fully understand.

Beyond the accidents of windows, walls, or work,
landscape, or my hands, something, or all, is
indivisible — centers everything
and hints of far rejoicing, because the earth,
good earth, is singing in my house:
my house is singing in the world,

and I am singing in my life. And yes,
my life sings out beyond me or my bones.
For all the words I sing are "yes," and "thank
you," for what it is I savor, yet hardly
understand. Here is my burning bush.
Is what I hear, "I AM!"?

1989

Hospitality

Cold winter midnight: I'm alone.
Wind sighs among shutters: snow
shifts, sags and falls in sudden thuds
from roof to heap and drift — snugging
the house and me. An ember flares
and dies. It's time for sleep.
I mark the page, take off my glasses,
settle down with thanks and prayers
for every living thing woven among
my other sleepy prayers. And then . . . a scritch,
scritch-scratching in the wall: silence, then
an even faster scritching starts again.

Once, I would have pounded floor
and wall to scare the thing away. Tonight
I bid you welcome, mouse: welcome mole
or hare. I hope you find the hearth-
stone and a bit of corn. The fire
is down . . . but all the bricks are warm.

1990

How on a Common Day
I Saw God's Back

Such small perfections as these stones
glistening in sunlight on the water's edge
give me excuse to rest and hold one for awhile.
So cool, so smoothed by its long history
it pleasures me this morning. I put it back
with blessings for all stones, then cross
the brook to walk in deeper woods.

Sheltering silence greets me, names me
sister: slips silken fingers in my own
as though we are familiars. Soon
there is quiet even in my bones
and stillness smoothing thoughts that had been hard
as rootballs needing water, air before repotting.

The trees are courteous. My eyes give thanks
for layered light sifted and sieved
through all their holy leaves. Petals
of light dance on the russet floor —
but there is more: a chickadee sings fee-bee,
fee-bee in such pure tones
I'll hear his song forever.

I must go back the way I came: resume
the common day. But when I reach the stones
they are in shadow now. Has morning gone?
And where? Hint of an answer comes —
borne on a breath of air, whispered
in weeds and grasses . . .

Then I remember what it was God said to Moses
once: "When my glory passes
I will set you in the hallowed rock,
cover you with my hand —
then take my hand away
so you may see my back." I read
that passage, "Beauty," sometimes.

I have seen God's back. His face
is another matter.

1991

Nurturing

Years later, when they sold the house,
they sent a box of things she'd saved:
drawings on manila paper, my first poems
awkwardly printed by a child of seven
then laced with scarlet yarn into a book.
(The joy of making ached in every finger
as I worked.) The *R* in FOR, the *N* in GRANDMA
on the cover had been smudged from trying
to erase their less than perfect shapes.
Even so, she found it wonderful. I was eleven
when she died. During the wake they tried
to comfort me. But choked between the torrent
of my tears, and sobs that wracked my skinny
body to the quick, I tried to say:
" — but she can't hug me anymore!"

So long ago that was . . . and yet, tonight
a certain softness in the light
here in the living-room reminds me of her house.
A large part of my soul was shaped there
in those rooms. Such sweet conspiracies
when we were home alone — like making ice cream
in a wooden tub, or, yes — a mouse
out of an old gray sock. And, oh, the stories
she would tell while kneading bread!

And best of all — the bed-time ritual. She'd wind
her magical Victrola then rock me while Caruso
or McCormack sang their hearts out for us. Once
I looked up when the music stopped and tears
were shining where her eyes were closed.
I didn't ask her why, but nestled down again —
knowing, without knowing, *some marvelous secret
lives at the heart of the world!*

1992

Light From Another Room

In that small room under the attic eaves
I never needed a nightlight, as I remember.
Stars shone at the window
where I said my prayers.
I'd lie and watch the great elm
playing hide and seek with them —
or simply hold them in its net of branches.
The dark was delicious then.
Even on rainy nights
the soft, warm quilt my Grandma made
Cozied the dark.

Or maybe it was the story read
before the lamp was dimmed:
the warm arms and the soft voice reading
all the wondrous words — a Fairy Tale,
or stories of Br'er Rabbit outsmarting
wily Fox. The world was always righted
in the end.

Some nights there were voices from
below: the Uncles come for cards.
Tinkle of glasses, dishes clattered,
stacked and put away . . . the register
sent more than Winter's heat up through the floor.

But when the night was dark, and silence
deeper still because some childhood fever
fretted sleep away . . . light from another room
shone where the door was left ajar. Never
intrusive, always there when needed.
Love waited there
lest I call out her name.

1993

Angels in the Summer Trees

Under the summer trees at sunset
it is not difficult to imagine
angels among the leaves, gathered along
the branches to watch the sun go down
from earthside after a busy day.

Guardians and messengers, and now our guests,
imagine them leaning above the nests
as birds pour pure enchantment on the evening
air. And then at moth-light bending to hear
those simple human sounds
that come at such an hour:

a mother calling children home for supper,
clicks of roller-skates on sidewalks,
a screen-door squeaking shut — a dog's bark
yippy with delight to find his master come.
Snatches of laughter, too, around a kitchen
table: grace being said.

When shadows fall on silent streets, sounds
of a piano — bell-like, beautiful . . .
and Mozart's music brings them messages
from home: our two worlds one at times like these.

Darkness deepens: from an upstairs window
bedtime-stories. A small child prays: "God bless
the whole wide world tonight . . ." A stir
of leaves (or is it wings?), there
in the nightgowned trees.
In any case, angels are there
to gather every prayer
and bring them home by heartfuls
up through the summer stars.

1994

About the Author

Eileen Lomasney is a writer and poet, often published and anthologized, whose work has found great appeal and recognition among many generations of readers.

Sister received her Bachelor's degree from The College of Saint Rose, Albany, New York, a Master of Arts from the University of Notre Dame, Notre Dame, Indiana, and has earned certificates in painting from the International Academy of Fine Arts, Salzburg, Austria, and in art history from the University of Rome, Italy where she studied under a Fulbright Grant.

For many years, Eileen taught kindergarten children, later becoming Associate Professor of Art at CSR. She was active in the Catholic Poetry Society, and is now a member of the American Poetry Society and of the Society of Children's Book Writers and Illustrators.

Born in Schenectady, New York on September 13, 1918, Eileen entered the Sisters of St. Joseph of Carondelet on September 8, 1936 – just shy of her eighteenth birthday. For the past several years, her religious community has provided her with time and support to pursue her vocation as a writer. In addition to her body of creative writing, she has written manuals on art appreciation for teaching professionals for *Art Education, Inc.*, Blauvelt, New York.

About the Cover Artist

Marion C. Honors has exhibited her singular gift in fine art and illustration in many one-woman and national group shows throughout the United States and in Europe. Her work can be found in private collections, churches and college campuses. The cover illustration represents just one of many collaborative efforts between writer and artist. Sister holds a Bachelor's degree from The College of Saint Rose, a Master of Arts from the University of Notre Dame and a Master of Fine Arts from Villa Schifanoia, Florence, Italy.

Inquiries and orders may be addressed to:

CANTICLE PRESS
371 Watervliet-Shaker Road
Latham, NY 12110-4741